PARIS 2024
Summer Olympics

Find our books at Amazon, Barnes & Nobles, Walmart, Books-A-Million, OverDrive, IngramSpark, Lulu and more!

Like, Share and Follow us on Facebook, Instagram, Twitter, Pinterest, YouTube, LinkedIn, Spotify, Apple Podcast and more!

www.SlothDreamsBooks.com

Copyright © 2024 by KeriAnne N. Jelinek
Illustrations by KeriAnne N. Jelinek
Cover Design by KeriAnne N. Jelinek

All rights reserved, including the right of reproduction in whole are in part in any form.
Sloth Dreams Books & Publishing, LLC. and colophon are registered trademarks of
Sloth Dreams Books & Publishing, LLC.

Published by Sloth Dreams Books & Publishing, LLC.
Sloth Dreams Children's Books
Pennsylvania, USA
www.SlothDreamsBooks.com

All Rights Reserved.

ISBN: 978-2-2760-7949-2

Except in the United States of America, this book is sold subject to the condition that it shall not, by way of trade or otherwise, be lent, re-sold, hired out, or otherwise circulated without the publisher's prior consent in any form of binding or cover other that in which it is published and without a similar condition including this condition being imposed on the subsequent purchaser.

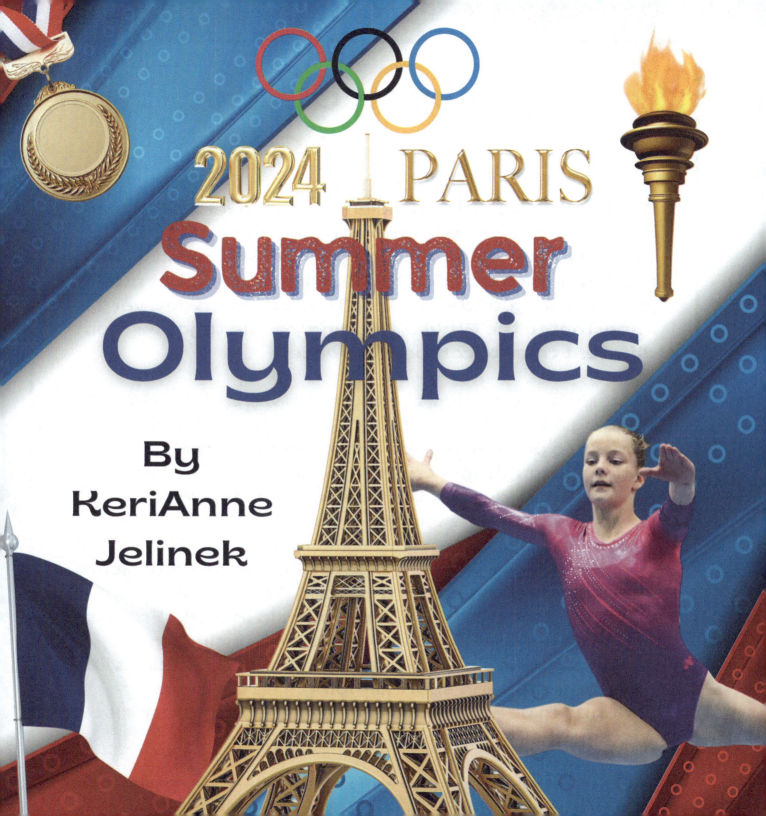

History of the Olympics

The Olympics began in ancient Greece over 2,700 years ago, in a place called Olympia. They were part of a festival to honor Zeus, the king of the Greek gods. The ancient games included running, long jump, shot put, javelin, boxing, and wrestling. These games were very important to the Greeks, bringing people together from different cities to compete in peace.

After many centuries, the Olympics were revived in 1896 by a Frenchman named Pierre de Coubertin. He wanted to promote peace and friendship among nations through sports. The modern Olympics have grown to include athletes from all over the world, competing in a wide variety of sports.

Today, the Summer Olympics are held every four years in different cities around the world. The upcoming Summer Olympics in 2024 will be held in Paris, France. They will feature many exciting sports, including athletics, swimming, gymnastics, and new additions like skateboarding and sport climbing. The Olympics continue to be a symbol of global unity and the spirit of friendly competition.

Summer Olympic Sports

- ARCHERY
- ARTISTIC GYMNASTICS
- ARTISTIC SWIMMING
- ATHLETICS
- BADMINTON
- BASKETBALL
- BASKETBALL 3X3
- BEACH VOLLEYBALL
- BOXING
- BREAKING
- CANOE SLALOM
- CANOE SPRINT
- CYCLING BMX FREESTYLE
- CYCLING BMX RACING
- CYCLING MOUNTAIN BIKE
- CYCLING ROAD
- CYCLING TRACK
- DIVING
- EQUESTRIAN
- FENCING
- FOOTBALL
- GOLF
- HANDBALL
- HOCKEY
- JUDO
- MARATHON SWIMMING
- MODERN PENTATHLON
- RHYTHMIC GYMNASTICS
- ROWING
- RUGBY SEVENS
- SAILING
- SHOOTING
- SKATEBOARDING
- SPORT CLIMBING
- SURFING
- SWIMMING
- TABLE TENNIS
- TAEKWONDO
- TENNIS
- TRAMPOLINE
- TRIATHLON
- VOLLEYBALL
- WATER POLO
- WEIGHTLIFTING
- WRESTLING

Archery

Description: Archery is the sport of shooting arrows at a target using a bow. Archers aim to hit the bullseye and score the highest points.

Famous Olympians: Kim Soo-Nyung from South Korea, who has won multiple Olympic medals.

Training: Archers practice their aim and concentration, often shooting hundreds of arrows a day. They also do strength training to improve their steadiness.

Artistic Gymnastics

Description: Artistic gymnastics involves performing routines on different apparatus like the vault, bars, beam, and floor.

Famous Olympians: Simone Biles, known for her incredible performances and numerous medals.

Training: Gymnasts train in flexibility, strength, and technique, practicing their routines many times to perfect each move.

Artistic Swimming

Description: Artistic swimming, also known as synchronized swimming, combines swimming, dance, and gymnastics, performed to music in the water.

Famous Olympians: Russia's Svetlana Romashina, a multiple gold medalist.

Training: Swimmers practice their routines both in and out of the water, focusing on timing, strength, and flexibility.

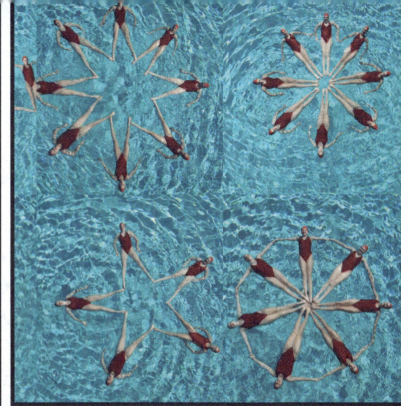

Athletics

Description: Athletics, also known as track and field, includes running, jumping, and throwing events.

Famous Olympians: Usain Bolt, the fastest man in the world.

Training: Athletes train in their specific event, focusing on speed, strength, and technique. They often follow a strict diet and exercise regimen.

Badminton

Description: Badminton is a fast-paced racket sport played with a shuttlecock. Players aim to hit the shuttlecock over the net into the opponent's court.

Famous Olympians: Lin Dan from China, a two-time Olympic champion.

Training: Players practice their strokes, footwork, and agility, often playing matches to improve their game strategy.

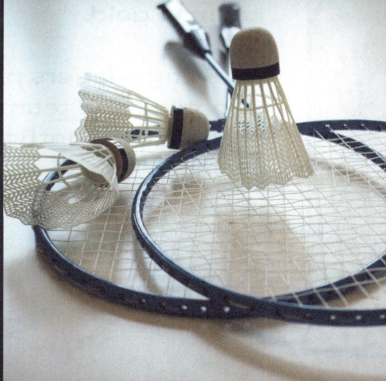

Basketball

Description: Basketball is a team sport where players aim to score points by shooting a ball through the opponent's hoop.

Famous Olympians: Michael Jordan, a legendary player who led the USA team to gold.

Training: Players practice dribbling, shooting, and teamwork. They also focus on strength and endurance training.

Basketball 3x3

Description: Basketball 3x3 is a faster-paced version of basketball with three players on each team, played on a half-court.

Famous Olympians: The USA team, strong contenders in both men's and women's categories.

Training: Similar to regular basketball but with a focus on speed, agility, and quick decision-making.

Beach Volleyball

Description: Beach volleyball is played on sand with teams of two. Players aim to hit the ball over the net and land it in the opponent's court.

Famous Olympians: Misty May-Treanor and Kerri Walsh Jennings, who have won multiple Olympic golds.

Training: Players practice their serves, spikes, and digs, often on sand to build strength and endurance.

Boxing

Description: Boxing is a combat sport where two opponents fight using their fists, aiming to score points or knock out the opponent.

Famous Olympians: Muhammad Ali, who won gold in 1960.

Training: Boxers train in punching techniques, footwork, and conditioning, often sparring with partners to improve their skills.

Breaking

Description: Breaking, also known as breakdancing, involves acrobatic dance moves and routines performed to music.

Famous Olympians: The Paris 2024 Games will feature breaking for the first time.

Training: Breakers practice their moves, spins, and freezes, focusing on strength, flexibility, and rhythm.

Canoe Slalom

Description: Canoe slalom is a timed event where athletes navigate a canoe or kayak through a course of hanging gates on a river.

Famous Olympians: Tony Estanguet from France, a three-time Olympic champion.

Training: Paddlers practice their techniques and maneuvers on rivers, focusing on speed and precision.

Canoe Sprint

Description: Canoe sprint is a race over calm water where athletes paddle their canoe or kayak over a set distance as fast as possible.

Famous Olympians: Birgit Fischer from Germany, who has won multiple gold medals.

Training: Athletes focus on paddling techniques, strength, and endurance, often doing long-distance paddling.

Cycling BMX Freestyle

Description: BMX freestyle involves performing tricks and stunts on a BMX bike in a park or on ramps.

Famous Olympians: Logan Martin from Australia, who won gold at Tokyo 2020.

Training: Riders practice their tricks and jumps, focusing on control and creativity, often in skateparks.

Cycling BMX Racing

Description: BMX racing is a fast-paced race over a dirt track with jumps and sharp turns.

Famous Olympians: Mariana Pajón from Colombia, a two-time Olympic gold medalist.

Training: Riders train on BMX tracks, focusing on speed, agility, and bike control.

Cycling Mountain Bike

Description: Mountain biking involves racing over rough terrain, including hills, rocks, and forests.

Famous Olympians: Julien Absalon from France, a two-time gold medalist.

Training: Cyclists train on various terrains, improving their endurance, technical skills, and bike handling.

Cycling Road

Description: Road cycling is a long-distance race on paved roads, often through cities and countryside.

Famous Olympians: Chris Froome, a Tour de France champion.

Training: Cyclists do long rides to build endurance, practice sprints, and work on their climbing skills.

Cycling Track

Description: Track cycling is a race on a velodrome, a specially designed cycling track, with various events like sprints and time trials.

Famous Olympians: Sir Chris Hoy from the UK, who has won multiple gold medals.

Training: Cyclists train on velodromes, focusing on speed, strategy, and bike handling.

Diving

Description: Diving involves jumping into water from a platform or springboard, performing acrobatics before entering the water.

Famous Olympians: Greg Louganis, a four-time gold medalist.

Training: Divers practice their jumps and twists, working on precision and body control. They also train in the gym for strength and flexibility.

Equestrian

Description: Equestrian sports involve horse riding, including dressage, show jumping, and eventing.

Famous Olympians: Charlotte Dujardin, a multiple gold medalist in dressage.

Training: Riders practice their skills on horseback, focusing on control, technique, and the partnership with their horse.

Fencing

Description: Fencing is a combat sport where opponents duel with swords, aiming to score points by touching their opponent with the blade.

Famous Olympians: Valentina Vezzali from Italy, who has won multiple gold medals.

Training: Fencers practice their moves, speed, and strategy, often sparring with partners to improve their skills.

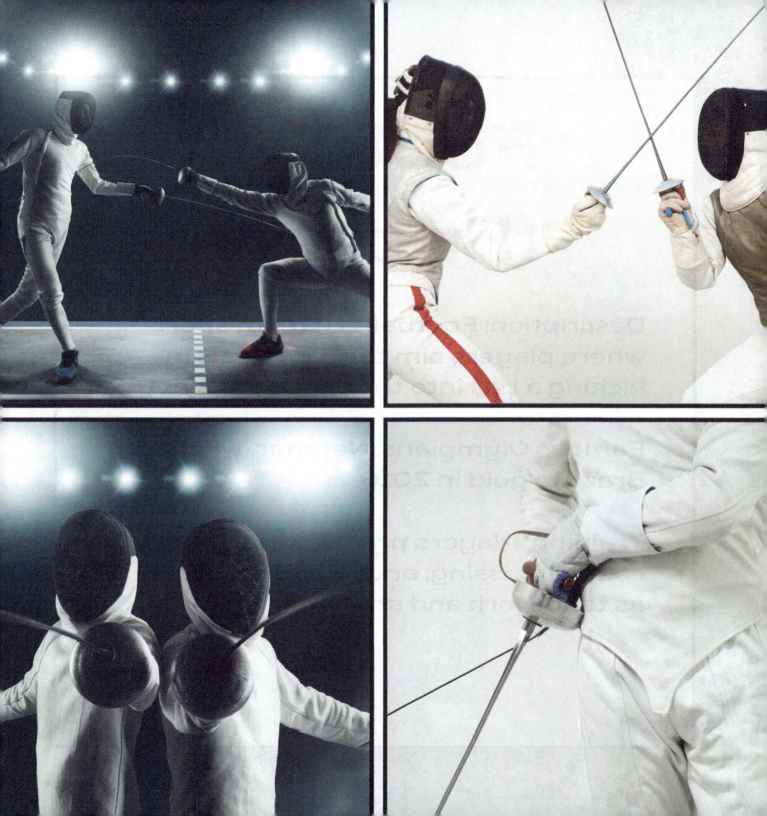

Football (Soccer)

Description: Football is a team sport where players aim to score goals by kicking a ball into the opponent's net.

Famous Olympians: Neymar, who led Brazil to gold in 2016.

Training: Players practice their ball control, passing, and shooting, as well as teamwork and strategy.

Golf

Description: Golf involves hitting a small ball into a series of holes on a course using various clubs, aiming for the fewest strokes.

Famous Olympians: Inbee Park, who won gold in 2016.

Training: Golfers practice their swings, putting, and strategy, often spending hours on the course and driving range.

Handball

Description: Handball is a team sport where players aim to score by throwing a ball into the opponent's goal.

Famous Olympians: France's men's and women's teams, known for their strong performances.

Training: Players practice their throwing, catching, and dribbling skills, as well as teamwork and strategy.

Hockey

Description: Field hockey is a team sport where players use sticks to hit a ball into the opponent's goal.

Famous Olympians: The Netherlands women's team, with multiple Olympic victories.

Training: Players practice their stick skills, passing, and teamwork, often doing drills and playing matches.

Judo

Description: Judo is a martial art where opponents aim to throw or pin each other to the ground using various techniques.

Famous Olympians: Tadahiro Nomura, a three-time Olympic champion.

Training: Judokas practice their throws and grappling techniques, as well as strength and conditioning.

Marathon Swimming

Description: Marathon swimming is a long-distance race in open water, covering a distance of 10 kilometers.

Famous Olympians: Sharon van Rouwendaal, who won gold in 2016.

Training: Swimmers train in open water, building endurance and practicing their pacing and navigation.

Modern Pentathlon

Description: Modern pentathlon includes five events: fencing, swimming, equestrian, shooting, and running.

Famous Olympians: Laura Asadauskaitė, a gold medalist from Lithuania.

Training: Athletes train in all five disciplines, balancing their time to improve in each event.

Rhythmic Gymnastics

Description: Rhythmic gymnastics involves performing graceful routines with apparatus like ribbons, hoops, balls, clubs, and ropes, all set to music.

Famous Olympians: Alina Kabaeva from Russia, known for her stunning performances.

Training: Gymnasts practice their routines and apparatus handling, focusing on flexibility, coordination, and timing. They also do a lot of strength and dance training.

Rowing

Description: Rowing is a sport where athletes race boats using oars, either individually or in teams.

Famous Olympians: Sir Steve Redgrave from the UK, who has won five gold medals.

Training: Rowers train on the water and in the gym, focusing on endurance, strength, and technique. They often practice rowing together to synchronize their strokes.

Rugby Sevens

Description: Rugby Sevens is a faster version of rugby with seven players on each team, played over two seven-minute halves.

Famous Olympians: The Fiji men's team, gold medalists in 2016 and 2021.

Training: Players train in running, tackling, and ball-handling skills, as well as strategy and teamwork. They also focus on speed and endurance.

Sailing

Description: Sailing involves racing boats on water, using wind to navigate through a course.

Famous Olympians: Ben Ainslie from the UK, a four-time Olympic gold medalist.

Training: Sailors practice on the water, learning to control their boats in different wind conditions. They also study navigation and weather patterns.

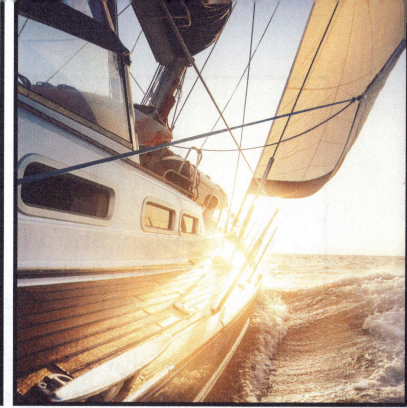

Shooting

Description: Shooting is a sport where athletes aim to hit targets with precision using rifles or pistols.

Famous Olympians: Niccolò Campriani from Italy, a multiple gold medalist.

Training: Shooters practice their aim, breath control, and focus. They also work on their strength and steadiness to handle the recoil of their firearms.

Skateboarding

Description: Skateboarding involves performing tricks and maneuvers on a skateboard, in either park or street events.

Famous Olympians: Nyjah Huston, known for his incredible skills in street skateboarding.

Training: Skaters practice their tricks and routines at skate parks, focusing on balance, agility, and creativity. They often spend hours perfecting each move.

Sport Climbing

Description: Sport climbing includes events like lead climbing, speed climbing, and bouldering, where athletes climb fixed routes on a wall.

Famous Olympians: Janja Garnbret from Slovenia, a gold medalist and climbing prodigy.

Training: Climbers practice on indoor climbing walls, improving their grip strength, technique, and problem-solving skills. They also do strength and endurance training.

Surfing

Description: Surfing involves riding waves on a surfboard, aiming to perform maneuvers and tricks.

Famous Olympians: Carissa Moore from the USA, a gold medalist and world champion.

Training: Surfers spend hours in the ocean, practicing their wave riding and maneuvers. They also do strength and balance exercises to improve their performance on the board.

Swimming

Description: Swimming includes various styles like freestyle, backstroke, breaststroke, and butterfly, raced over different distances.

Famous Olympians: Michael Phelps, the most decorated Olympian of all time.

Training: Swimmers train in the pool, doing laps and drills to improve their technique and endurance. They also do strength training and flexibility exercises.

Table Tennis

Description: Table tennis, also known as ping pong, is played with small paddles and a lightweight ball, aiming to score points by hitting the ball over the net.

Famous Olympians: Ma Long from China, a multiple gold medalist.

Training: Players practice their serves, spins, and rallies, focusing on quick reflexes and strategy. They often play matches to hone their competitive skills.

Taekwondo

Description: Taekwondo is a martial art that focuses on high, fast kicks and powerful punches.

Famous Olympians: Jade Jones from the UK, a two-time Olympic gold medalist.

Training: Practitioners train in kicking techniques, sparring, and forms. They also focus on flexibility, strength, and agility.

Tennis

Description: Tennis is a racket sport where players hit a ball over a net, aiming to score points by making the ball land in the opponent's court.

Famous Olympians: Serena Williams, a four-time Olympic gold medalist.

Training: Players practice their serves, volleys, and groundstrokes. They also focus on agility, endurance, and strategic play.

Trampoline

Description: Trampoline gymnastics involves performing acrobatic moves and routines while bouncing on a trampoline.

Famous Olympians: Dong Dong from China, a multiple medalist in trampoline gymnastics.

Training: Gymnasts practice their routines on trampolines, focusing on timing, technique, and precision. They also do strength and flexibility exercises.

Triathlon

Description: Triathlon is a multi-sport event that includes swimming, cycling, and running.

Famous Olympians: Alistair Brownlee from the UK, a two-time Olympic gold medalist.

Training: Triathletes train in all three disciplines, often doing long-distance workouts to build endurance and practicing transitions between events.

Volleyball

Description: Volleyball is a team sport where players aim to score points by hitting a ball over a net into the opponent's court.

Famous Olympians: The Brazilian men's and women's teams, known for their strong performances.

Training: Players practice their serves, spikes, and blocks, focusing on teamwork and communication. They also do strength and agility training.

Water Polo

Description: Water polo is a team sport played in a pool, where players aim to score goals by throwing a ball into the opponent's net.

Famous Olympians: The Hungarian men's team, with a storied history of success.

Training: Players practice their swimming, ball handling, and shooting skills. They also focus on endurance and teamwork.

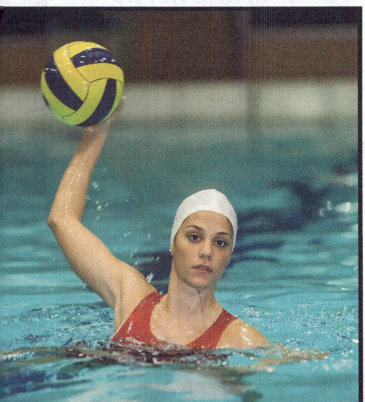

Weightlifting

Description: Weightlifting involves lifting heavy weights in two events: the snatch and the clean and jerk.

Famous Olympians: Naim Süleymanoğlu from Turkey, known as "The Pocket Hercules" for his incredible lifts.

Training: Lifters train with weights, focusing on strength, technique, and explosive power. They also follow a strict diet and recovery regimen.

Wrestling

Description: Wrestling is a combat sport where opponents aim to pin each other to the mat or score points through holds and maneuvers.

Famous Olympians: Kaori Icho from Japan, a four-time Olympic gold medalist.

Training: Wrestlers practice their techniques and spar with partners. They also focus on strength, agility, and conditioning to maintain peak physical fitness.

Paris Summer Olympics 2024

The 2024 Summer Olympics will be held in Paris, France, a city renowned for its rich history, stunning architecture, and cultural landmarks. This will be the third time Paris hosts the Olympics, previously holding the Games in 1900 and 1924. Known as the "City of Light," Paris will provide a magnificent backdrop for the international sporting event, combining its iconic sites with the spirit of athletic excellence.

The Olympic venues are strategically scattered across the city, ensuring that 80% of the competition sites are within 10 kilometers of the Olympic and Paralympic Village in the heart of Paris. Spectators can expect to see events in breathtaking locations such as the Eiffel Tower, which will host beach volleyball, and the Champs-Élysées, which will be part of the cycling routes.

Summer Olympics
Paris 2024

The 2024 Olympics will not only highlight Paris but also other French cities like Lyon and Marseille, expanding the celebration of sports across the nation. The diverse venues range from the historic Stade de France for athletics to the Grand Palais for fencing, showcasing France's blend of tradition and modernity.

With around 15,000 athletes from over 200 countries expected to compete, the Games will be a global spectacle of sportsmanship and unity. Paris is preparing to welcome millions of visitors, promising a vibrant and festive atmosphere throughout the event. The city's excellent public transport and extensive hospitality options will ensure that visitors can easily navigate and enjoy their Olympic experience.

The Summer Olympics in Paris 2024 will feature these sports, bringing together athletes from around the world to compete in historic venues across the city. It's a chance to see incredible performances and celebrate the spirit of the Olympics in the beautiful city of Paris.

PARIS 2024
Summer
Olympics

Made in the USA
Coppell, TX
12 July 2024